Smart Money Moves For Young Adults:

The Modern Teen's Guide to Budgeting, Savings, And Smart Investing (Essential Life Skills To Build Your Dreams)

BY
Franklin Abernathy

CONTENTS

INTRODUCTION 4

Part I: 11
Building a Strong Financial Foundation 11

Chapter 01 12
Understanding Your Money Personality 12
Chapter 02 18
Budgeting Basics: Making Every Dollar Count 18
Chapter 03 26
Saving for Your Goals 26
Chapter 04 33
Earning Extra Cash 33

Part II: 42
Mastering the Art of Spending 42

Chapter 05 43
Smart Shopping and Saving 43
Chapter 06 51
Dining Out and Entertainment on a Budget 51
Chapter 07 58
Managing Debt and Building Credit 58

Part III: 66
Investing for Your Future 66

Chapter 08 67
Investing Basics: Understanding the Market 67

Chapter 09 73
Stocks, Bonds, and Mutual Funds: A Beginner's Guide .73
Chapter 10 82
Retirement Planning: Starting Early Pays Off 82

Part IV: 89
Financial Wellness and Beyond 89

Chapter 11 90
Financial Literacy and Beyond: Building a Strong Future 90
Chapter 12 96
Navigating Financial Challenges and Building Resilience 96

CONCLUSION 101

INTRODUCTION

Understanding the Importance of Financial Literacy

Financial literacy is more crucial today than ever before. As young adults embark on their journey towards independence, understanding how to manage money becomes a vital skill. Financial literacy involves knowing how to budget, save, invest, and spend wisely. These skills can lead to a more secure and prosperous future, reducing stress and opening up opportunities for growth and success.

Why Financial Literacy Matters

- **Empowerment**: Financial literacy empowers young adults to make informed decisions about their money.
- **Security**: With proper money management, individuals can achieve financial stability and security.
- **Opportunities**: Knowledge about finances opens up investment opportunities and allows for smart financial planning.
- **Avoiding Debt**: Understanding financial principles helps in avoiding unnecessary debt and managing existing debt effectively.
- **Future Planning**: It enables effective planning for the future, including buying a home, starting a business, or saving for retirement.

The Unique Challenges of Money Management for Young Adults

Young adults face unique challenges when it comes to managing money. These challenges can stem from limited financial education, peer pressure, and the transition from dependence to independence. Recognizing these challenges is the first step toward overcoming them.

Common Challenges

- **Lack of Financial Education**: Many young adults receive little to no formal education on managing finances.
- **Peer Pressure**: The desire to fit in can lead to overspending on non-essential items.
- **Student Loans**: Managing student debt can be overwhelming and impact financial stability.
- **Limited Income**: Entry-level jobs often come with lower salaries, making budgeting crucial.
- **Digital Temptations**: Online shopping and the ease of digital payments can lead to impulsive buying.

Addressing the Challenges

- **Education**: Seek out resources and educational opportunities to learn about finances.
- **Budgeting**: Create a realistic budget and stick to it.
- **Debt Management**: Develop a plan to manage and pay off student loans.
- **Saving**: Prioritize saving, even if it's a small amount each month.
- **Mindful Spending**: Be aware of spending habits and avoid impulsive purchases.

Setting Financial Goals: Short-Term, Medium-Term, and Long-Term

Setting clear financial goals is essential for effective money management. Goals give direction and motivation, helping to prioritize spending and saving.

Short-Term Goals (0-1 year)

- **Emergency Fund**: Build an emergency fund to cover 3-6 months of living expenses.
- **Debt Repayment**: Pay off high-interest debt such as credit cards.
- **Budgeting**: Create and stick to a monthly budget.

Medium-Term Goals (1-5 years)

- **Savings Milestones**: Set targets for savings accounts, such as saving for a car or a major trip.
- **Career Development**: Invest in further education or training to advance in your career.
- **Investment Beginnings**: Start investing in a retirement account or other investment opportunities.

Long-Term Goals (5+ years)

- **Homeownership**: Save for a down payment on a house.
- **Retirement Planning**: Consistently contribute to retirement accounts.
- **Major Investments**: Plan for large investments like starting a business or further education.

Building a Strong Financial Foundation: The Why and How

A strong financial foundation is crucial for long-term financial health. This involves creating a stable base upon which to build wealth and security.

The Why

- **Stability**: A strong financial foundation provides stability and peace of mind.
- **Growth**: It allows for growth opportunities, such as investing and expanding income sources.
- **Security**: Reduces the risk of financial emergencies and crises.

The How

- **Budgeting**: Track income and expenses to create a balanced budget.
- **Saving**: Prioritize saving a portion of income regularly.
- **Investing**: Begin investing early to take advantage of compound interest.
- **Insurance**: Secure health, auto, and life insurance to protect against unforeseen events.
- **Debt Management**: Keep debt levels manageable and work towards paying off existing debt.

Overcoming Financial Anxiety and Building Confidence

Financial anxiety is a common issue, especially among young adults. Overcoming this anxiety is crucial for effective money management and financial success.

Understanding Financial Anxiety

- **Causes**: Financial anxiety can stem from lack of knowledge, debt, and economic uncertainty.
- **Symptoms**: Symptoms include stress, avoidance of financial tasks, and feelings of helplessness.

Strategies to Overcome Financial Anxiety

- **Education**: Increase financial knowledge through books, courses, and online resources.
- **Planning**: Create a detailed financial plan to provide a clear path forward.
- **Support**: Seek advice from financial advisors or mentors.
- **Mindfulness**: Practice mindfulness and stress-reduction techniques.
- **Small Steps**: Take small, manageable steps towards financial goals to build confidence.

Building Financial Confidence

- **Celebrate Milestones**: Acknowledge and celebrate financial achievements, no matter how small.
- **Stay Informed**: Keep up-to-date with financial news and trends.
- **Seek Feedback**: Regularly review financial plans and seek feedback from trusted sources.
- **Stay Positive**: Maintain a positive mindset and focus on long-term goals.

In conclusion, financial literacy is a critical skill for young adults. By understanding the importance of financial literacy, addressing unique challenges, setting clear financial goals, building a strong financial foundation, and overcoming financial anxiety, young adults can take control of their financial future. This guide aims to provide actionable steps and detailed information to help young adults navigate the complexities of money management and achieve financial success.

Part I: Building a Strong Financial Foundation

Chapter 01

Understanding Your Money Personality

Understanding your money personality is the first step towards building a strong financial foundation. Your attitudes, beliefs, and behaviors regarding money significantly influence how you manage your finances. By identifying your money personality, you can tailor your financial strategies to better align with your natural tendencies, making it easier to stick to your financial goals.

Identifying Your Spending Habits

Your spending habits reveal a lot about your money personality. Some people are natural savers, while others are spenders. Recognizing your tendencies helps in creating a balanced approach to money management.

Steps to Identify Spending Habits

1. **Reflect on Past Spending**: Look at your spending patterns over the past few months. Note where you tend to spend the most money and what triggers these expenditures.
2. **Categorize Expenses**: Break down your expenses into categories such as necessities, entertainment, dining, and discretionary spending.
3. **Identify Patterns**: Look for patterns in your spending. Are there specific times, emotions, or situations that lead to higher spending?
4. **Assess Needs vs. Wants**: Determine which expenses are essential and which are based on wants or impulses.

Recognizing the Impact of Peer Pressure on Spending

Peer pressure can significantly influence your spending habits, especially as a young adult. The desire to fit in and keep up with friends can lead to unnecessary expenses and financial strain.

Understanding Peer Pressure

- **Social Influence**: Friends and social groups can impact your spending decisions, pushing you towards purchases you might not otherwise make.
- **Comparison**: Social media and peer comparisons can create unrealistic expectations about lifestyle and spending.
- **FOMO**: Fear of missing out (FOMO) can lead to spending on events, gadgets, and trends to stay in the loop.

Strategies to Manage Peer Pressure

1. **Set Boundaries**: Be clear about your financial goals and set boundaries to avoid overspending.
2. **Communicate**: Talk to your friends about your financial priorities. True friends will understand and support your goals.
3. **Seek Support**: Find friends or groups that share your financial values and can offer support and encouragement.
4. **Mindfulness**: Practice mindfulness to stay aware of your spending triggers and make conscious choices.

Creating a Spending Journal to Track Expenses

A spending journal is an effective tool to understand your spending habits and identify areas for improvement. It provides a clear picture of where your money is going and helps you make informed financial decisions.

How to Create a Spending Journal

1. **Choose a Method**: Decide whether you prefer a physical notebook, a spreadsheet, or a mobile app to track your expenses.
2. **Record Daily**: Write down every expense daily, including small purchases like coffee or snacks.
3. **Categorize Expenses**: Organize your entries by categories such as groceries, entertainment, transportation, etc.
4. **Review Regularly**: At the end of each week or month, review your entries to identify spending patterns and areas where you can cut back.

The Importance of Delayed Gratification

Delayed gratification is the ability to resist the temptation for an immediate reward and wait for a later, often better, reward. This skill is crucial for effective money management and achieving long-term financial goals.

Benefits of Delayed Gratification

- **Savings Growth**: By delaying purchases, you can save more money and take advantage of compound interest.
- **Reduced Impulse Spending**: It helps in avoiding impulsive buys that can derail your budget.
- **Goal Achievement**: Focusing on long-term goals over short-term desires leads to greater financial success and satisfaction.

How to Practice Delayed Gratification

1. **Set Clear Goals**: Having clear financial goals makes it easier to prioritize long-term rewards over immediate gratification.
2. **Create a Waiting Period**: Implement a waiting period for non-essential purchases to ensure they are necessary and within your budget.
3. **Reward Yourself**: Allow occasional rewards for meeting financial milestones to stay motivated.
4. **Visualize Success**: Visualize the benefits of achieving your long-term financial goals to reinforce the practice of delayed gratification.

Setting Realistic Financial Expectations

Setting realistic financial expectations is essential for maintaining motivation and achieving your goals. Unrealistic expectations can lead to frustration, while achievable goals build confidence and momentum.

Steps to Set Realistic Expectations

1. **Assess Your Current Situation**: Understand your current financial status, including income, expenses, and debt.
2. **Define Your Goals**: Set clear, specific financial goals that are achievable within your current circumstances.
3. **Break Down Goals**: Divide long-term goals into smaller, manageable steps to track progress and stay motivated.
4. **Be Flexible**: Adjust your goals as needed based on changes in your financial situation or priorities.
5. **Monitor Progress**: Regularly review your progress and celebrate small victories along the way.

Examples of Realistic Financial Goals

- **Short-Term**: Save $500 for an emergency fund within three months.
- **Medium-Term**: Pay off $5,000 in credit card debt within two years.
- **Long-Term**: Save $20,000 for a down payment on a house within five years.

By understanding your money personality, recognizing the impact of peer pressure, tracking your expenses, practicing delayed gratification, and setting realistic financial expectations, you can build a strong financial foundation. These steps will empower you to make informed decisions, achieve your financial goals, and enjoy a more secure and prosperous future.

Chapter 02

Budgeting Basics: Making Every Dollar Count

Budgeting is the cornerstone of financial stability and success. It involves planning and controlling where your money goes, ensuring that every dollar is used effectively. This chapter will guide you through the basics of budgeting, including different budgeting methods, tools, and techniques to track your income and expenses.

Defining Budgeting and Its Importance

What is Budgeting?

Budgeting is the process of creating a plan to spend your money. This spending plan, or budget, helps you determine in advance whether you will have enough money to do the things you need to do or would like to do.

Why is Budgeting Important?

- **Financial Control**: Budgeting gives you control over your money, allowing you to make informed spending decisions.
- **Goal Achievement**: It helps you allocate resources towards your financial goals, such as saving for a vacation, paying off debt, or building an emergency fund.
- **Avoiding Debt**: By planning your expenses, you can avoid overspending and accumulating debt.
- **Stress Reduction**: Knowing where your money goes reduces financial stress and anxiety.
- **Preparedness**: A budget prepares you for unexpected expenses by ensuring you have funds set aside for emergencies.

The 50/30/20 Budgeting Rule

One popular and straightforward budgeting method is the 50/30/20 rule. This rule divides your after-tax income into three categories: needs, wants, and savings.

Breakdown of the 50/30/20 Rule

50% for Needs: Allocate half of your income to necessities. These are essential expenses that you must pay to live and work. Examples include:

- Rent or mortgage payments
- Utilities
- Groceries
- Transportation
- Insurance
- Minimum debt payments

30% for Wants: Set aside 30% of your income for discretionary spending. These are non-essential expenses that you enjoy but can live without. Examples include:

- Dining out
- Entertainment
- Hobbies
- Travel
- Subscription services

20% for Savings and Debt Repayment: The remaining 20% should go towards savings and paying off debt. This category includes:

- Emergency fund contributions

- Retirement savings
- Extra debt payments (beyond the minimum)
- Investments

Advantages of the 50/30/20 Rule

- **Simplicity**: It provides a clear and simple framework for managing your money.
- **Flexibility**: The rule allows for flexibility in how you spend and save within each category.
- **Balance**: It encourages a balanced approach to spending and saving, ensuring you cover essential needs while also enjoying your wants and securing your future.

Creating a Personalized Budget

While the 50/30/20 rule is a great starting point, creating a personalized budget tailored to your specific financial situation and goals can be more effective.

Steps to Create a Personalized Budget

1. **Calculate Your Income**: Determine your total monthly income after taxes. Include all sources of income, such as salary, freelance work, and side hustles.
2. **List Your Expenses**: Make a comprehensive list of your monthly expenses. Divide them into fixed expenses (rent, utilities) and variable expenses (groceries, entertainment).
3. **Categorize Expenses**: Group your expenses into categories similar to the 50/30/20 rule, but adjust the percentages based on your unique situation.

4. **Set Financial Goals**: Define your short-term, medium-term, and long-term financial goals. Allocate funds towards achieving these goals.
5. **Allocate Funds**: Assign a specific amount to each expense category. Ensure your total expenses do not exceed your total income.
6. **Adjust and Optimize**: Review your budget regularly and adjust as needed. Look for areas where you can cut back to increase savings or pay off debt faster.

Tips for Creating an Effective Budget

- **Be Realistic**: Set realistic spending limits based on your actual income and expenses.
- **Prioritize**: Focus on essential expenses and savings before discretionary spending.
- **Stay Flexible**: Be prepared to adjust your budget as your financial situation changes.
- **Track Spending**: Regularly monitor your spending to ensure you stay within your budget.

Using Budgeting Apps and Tools

Technology can simplify the budgeting process. There are numerous budgeting apps and tools available that can help you track your income, expenses, and financial goals.

Popular Budgeting Apps

- **Mint**: Mint is a free app that connects to your bank accounts, tracks your spending, and helps you create and stick to a budget.

- **YNAB (You Need a Budget)**: YNAB is a paid app that focuses on proactive budgeting and encourages you to allocate every dollar towards a specific purpose.
- **PocketGuard**: PocketGuard links to your financial accounts and shows you how much disposable income you have after covering bills and necessities.
- **EveryDollar**: Created by financial expert Dave Ramsey, EveryDollar helps you create a zero-based budget, where every dollar is assigned a job.
- **Goodbudget**: Goodbudget uses the envelope budgeting method to help you allocate funds to different categories and track spending.

Benefits of Budgeting Apps

- **Automation**: Automatically track income and expenses, reducing manual effort.
- **Insights**: Provide insights and visualizations of your spending habits.
- **Goal Setting**: Help you set and monitor financial goals.
- **Reminders**: Send reminders for bill payments and savings contributions.
- **Synchronization**: Sync across multiple devices for easy access and updates.

Tracking Income and Expenses Regularly

Consistently tracking your income and expenses is crucial to maintaining an effective budget. It helps you stay on top of your financial situation and make informed adjustments as needed.

Methods for Tracking

- **Manual Tracking**: Use a spreadsheet or notebook to record your income and expenses manually. This method requires discipline but offers complete control over the tracking process.
- **Budgeting Apps**: Utilize budgeting apps to automate tracking and get real-time updates on your spending.
- **Bank Statements**: Regularly review your bank statements to monitor transactions and ensure they align with your budget.

Tips for Effective Tracking

- **Be Consistent**: Record transactions as they occur to avoid forgetting or overlooking expenses.
- **Review Regularly**: Set aside time each week or month to review your income and expenses, ensuring you stay within your budget.
- **Adjust as Needed**: Be flexible and adjust your budget based on actual spending patterns and changing financial circumstances.
- **Stay Disciplined**: Stick to your budget and resist the temptation to overspend, especially in discretionary categories.

By understanding the basics of budgeting, implementing a structured budgeting method like the 50/30/20 rule, creating a personalized budget, leveraging budgeting apps and tools, and consistently tracking your income and expenses, you can make every dollar count. These steps will empower you to take control of your finances, achieve your financial goals, and build a strong financial foundation for the future.

Chapter 03
Saving for Your Goals

Saving money is a crucial aspect of financial health and achieving your financial goals. This chapter will explore the power of compound interest, how to set specific savings goals, the benefits of creating multiple savings accounts, the importance of automating savings, and strategies to overcome common saving obstacles.

The Power of Compound Interest

What is Compound Interest?

Compound interest is the interest earned on the initial principal and the interest that has been added to it over time. In other words, you earn interest on both the money you save and the interest that money generates.

How Compound Interest Works

- **Initial Principal**: The original amount of money you save or invest.
- **Interest Rate**: The percentage at which your money grows annually.
- **Compounding Periods**: The frequency with which interest is applied to your account (e.g., monthly, quarterly, annually).

Example

Imagine you save $1,000 at an annual interest rate of 5%, compounded annually:

- After 1 year: $1,000 + ($1,000 * 0.05) = $1,050
- After 2 years: $1,050 + ($1,050 * 0.05) = $1,102.50
- After 10 years: $1,000 * (1 + 0.05)^10 = $1,628.89

The Benefits of Compound Interest

- **Exponential Growth**: Your savings grow faster over time due to the compounding effect.
- **Early Start Advantage**: The earlier you start saving, the more time your money has to grow.
- **Passive Income**: Compound interest generates passive income, which can significantly contribute to achieving your financial goals.

Setting Specific Savings Goals

Importance of Specific Savings Goals

Having specific savings goals provides direction and motivation, making it easier to stay disciplined and focused.

Types of Savings Goals

- **Short-Term Goals**: Goals you plan to achieve within a year, such as saving for a vacation, a new gadget, or a small emergency fund.
- **Medium-Term Goals**: Goals you aim to achieve within 1-5 years, like saving for a car, a wedding, or further education.
- **Long-Term Goals**: Goals that take more than five years to achieve, such as saving for a house down payment, retirement, or children's education.

How to Set Specific Savings Goals

1. **Define the Goal**: Clearly state what you are saving for and why it is important.

2. **Determine the Amount**: Calculate how much money you need to save to achieve the goal.
3. **Set a Timeline**: Establish a realistic timeframe to reach your savings goal.
4. **Break It Down**: Divide the total amount by the number of months or weeks in your timeline to determine how much you need to save regularly.

Example

Goal: Save $5,000 for a vacation in two years.

- Timeline: 24 months
- Monthly Savings Needed: $5,000 / 24 = $208.33

Creating Multiple Savings Accounts

Benefits of Multiple Savings Accounts

- **Organization**: Separate accounts for different goals help you stay organized and focused.
- **Clear Progress**: It is easier to track progress towards each goal.
- **Reduced Temptation**: Keeping funds separate minimizes the temptation to dip into savings for non-goal-related expenses.

Types of Savings Accounts

- **Emergency Fund Account**: An account dedicated to covering unexpected expenses.
- **Specific Goal Accounts**: Accounts for individual goals such as vacations, car purchases, or home down payments.

- **High-Interest Savings Account**: An account for long-term goals where money can grow with compound interest.

How to Manage Multiple Savings Accounts

1. **Identify Your Goals**: Determine the specific goals you want to save for.
2. **Open Accounts**: Open separate savings accounts for each goal. Many banks offer the option to create multiple sub-accounts.
3. **Allocate Funds**: Allocate a portion of your income to each account based on your savings plan.
4. **Monitor Progress**: Regularly review each account to ensure you are on track to meet your goals.

Automating Savings

The Importance of Automating Savings

Automating your savings helps you stay consistent and disciplined, ensuring you regularly contribute to your savings goals without forgetting or being tempted to spend the money elsewhere.

How to Automate Savings

1. **Set Up Automatic Transfers**: Arrange for automatic transfers from your checking account to your savings accounts on a regular basis (e.g., monthly, bi-weekly).
2. **Direct Deposit**: If your employer offers direct deposit, allocate a portion of your paycheck to go directly into your savings accounts.

3. **Use Savings Apps**: Some apps automatically round up your purchases and transfer the spare change into your savings account.

Benefits of Automating Savings

- **Consistency**: Ensures regular contributions to your savings accounts.
- **Simplicity**: Simplifies the savings process, reducing the need for manual transfers.
- **Discipline**: Helps you stick to your savings plan and avoid impulsive spending.

Overcoming Saving Obstacles

Common Obstacles to Saving

- **Limited Income**: Struggling to save due to low income or high expenses.
- **Unexpected Expenses**: Emergency expenses that deplete your savings.
- **Lack of Discipline**: Difficulty staying consistent with savings contributions.
- **Temptation to Spend**: Temptation to spend money on non-essential items.

Strategies to Overcome Saving Obstacles

1. **Budgeting**: Create and stick to a budget that prioritizes savings.
2. **Reduce Expenses**: Identify areas where you can cut back on spending to free up money for savings.

3. **Increase Income**: Explore opportunities to increase your income, such as side jobs or freelance work.
4. **Emergency Fund**: Build an emergency fund to cover unexpected expenses without depleting your other savings.
5. **Set Smaller Goals**: Start with smaller, more manageable savings goals to build momentum and confidence.
6. **Stay Motivated**: Regularly remind yourself of your savings goals and the benefits of achieving them.
7. **Accountability**: Share your savings goals with a trusted friend or family member who can help keep you accountable.

By understanding the power of compound interest, setting specific savings goals, creating multiple savings accounts, automating your savings, and overcoming common obstacles, you can effectively save for your financial goals. These strategies will help you build a solid savings plan, stay motivated, and achieve the financial security and success you desire.

Chapter 04
Earning Extra Cash

Increasing your income is an essential step in achieving financial stability and accelerating progress toward your financial goals. Whether you are saving for a specific purpose or trying to pay down debt faster, earning extra cash can make a significant difference. This chapter will explore various ways to earn additional income, including part-time job opportunities, freelancing and gig economy options, online money-making ventures, turning hobbies into income, and saving tips for extra income.

Exploring Part-Time Job Opportunities

Benefits of Part-Time Jobs

- **Additional Income**: Boost your earnings without a long-term commitment.
- **Skill Development**: Gain new skills and experiences that can enhance your resume.
- **Networking**: Meet new people and expand your professional network.
- **Flexibility**: Many part-time jobs offer flexible hours that can fit around your primary commitments.

Types of Part-Time Jobs

1. **Retail**: Working in a store, assisting customers, and managing inventory.
2. **Food Service**: Jobs in restaurants, cafes, or catering services as a server, host, or cook.
3. **Tutoring**: Offering tutoring services in subjects you excel in.
4. **Childcare**: Babysitting or working at a daycare center.

5. **Delivery Services**: Delivering food or packages for companies like DoorDash, Uber Eats, or Amazon Flex.
6. **Administrative Work**: Assisting with clerical tasks in offices or remotely.

How to Find Part-Time Jobs

- **Job Boards**: Use online job boards like Indeed, Glassdoor, and LinkedIn to search for part-time opportunities.
- **Local Listings**: Check local classifieds, community bulletin boards, and social media groups.
- **Networking**: Ask friends, family, and acquaintances if they know of any part-time openings.
- **Company Websites**: Visit the careers pages of companies you're interested in working for.

Freelancing and Gig Economy Options

What is Freelancing?

Freelancing involves offering your skills and services on a project-by-project basis rather than being employed full-time by one company. It provides flexibility and the potential to earn a higher income by working with multiple clients.

Popular Freelancing Platforms

- **Upwork**: A platform where freelancers can find projects across various fields, including writing, design, programming, and marketing.

- **Fiverr**: Offers a marketplace for freelancers to offer services starting at $5, covering a wide range of categories.
- **Freelancer**: Connects freelancers with businesses looking for talent in multiple disciplines.
- **Toptal**: Focuses on connecting top freelancers with high-quality clients in tech, design, and finance.

Types of Freelancing Gigs

- **Writing and Editing**: Content creation, copywriting, blog writing, and proofreading.
- **Graphic Design**: Creating logos, marketing materials, and website designs.
- **Programming and Web Development**: Building websites, apps, and software solutions.
- **Digital Marketing**: Managing social media accounts, SEO, and online advertising.
- **Virtual Assistance**: Providing administrative support remotely.
- **Consulting**: Offering expert advice in areas such as business, finance, and technology.

Benefits of the Gig Economy

- **Flexibility**: Choose when and where you work.
- **Variety**: Work on different projects and with various clients.
- **Potential for High Earnings**: Set your rates and take on multiple projects to increase your income.
- **Skill Enhancement**: Continuously develop and refine your skills through diverse projects.

Online Money-Making Ventures

Online Surveys and Market Research

Participating in online surveys and market research studies can provide a simple way to earn extra money. Companies pay for consumer opinions to improve their products and services.

Popular Survey Sites

- **Swagbucks**: Earn points (Swagbucks) for taking surveys, watching videos, and shopping online, which can be redeemed for gift cards or cash.
- **Survey Junkie**: Complete surveys to earn points, which can be exchanged for cash or e-gift cards.
- **Vindale Research**: Get paid for sharing your opinions on products and services.

Selling Products Online

Selling products online can be a profitable venture. You can sell handmade crafts, vintage items, or even unused items from around your home.

Platforms for Selling Products

- **eBay**: Sell almost anything to a global audience through auctions or fixed-price listings.
- **Etsy**: A marketplace for handmade, vintage, and unique goods.
- **Amazon**: Use Amazon's platform to sell products directly to consumers.
- **Facebook Marketplace**: Sell items locally without fees.

Affiliate Marketing

Affiliate marketing involves promoting products or services and earning a commission for each sale made through your referral link.

Steps to Start Affiliate Marketing

1. **Choose a Niche**: Select a specific area of interest or expertise.
2. **Join Affiliate Programs**: Sign up for affiliate programs from companies like Amazon Associates, ShareASale, or Commission Junction.
3. **Promote Products**: Use a blog, social media, or email marketing to promote products and include your affiliate links.
4. **Earn Commissions**: Receive commissions for every sale made through your referral links.

Turning Hobbies into Income

Identifying Marketable Hobbies

Many hobbies have the potential to generate income. Consider what you enjoy doing and how it can be monetized.

Examples of Marketable Hobbies

- **Photography**: Sell your photos online, offer photography services for events, or create prints for sale.
- **Crafting**: Create handmade items such as jewelry, candles, or home decor to sell on platforms like Etsy.

- **Writing**: Write and sell eBooks, start a blog with monetization options, or offer freelance writing services.
- **Fitness**: Become a personal trainer, offer online fitness classes, or create fitness-related content.
- **Gardening**: Sell homegrown produce, plants, or gardening services.

Steps to Monetize Your Hobby

1. **Evaluate Demand**: Research the market to determine if there is demand for your hobby-related products or services.
2. **Create a Plan**: Develop a business plan outlining your goals, target audience, and marketing strategy.
3. **Build a Brand**: Establish a brand identity, including a name, logo, and online presence.
4. **Market Your Hobby**: Use social media, online marketplaces, and local events to promote your products or services.
5. **Seek Feedback**: Continuously improve your offerings based on customer feedback.

Saving Tips for Extra Income

Prioritizing Savings

When you earn extra income, it is essential to prioritize saving a portion of it to achieve your financial goals faster.

Strategies to Save Extra Income

- **Automate Savings**: Set up automatic transfers to your savings accounts whenever you receive extra income.
- **Create a Separate Account**: Open a dedicated account for extra income to avoid mixing it with your regular funds.
- **Set Clear Goals**: Define what you want to achieve with your extra income, such as building an emergency fund, paying off debt, or saving for a big purchase.
- **Track Progress**: Monitor your savings progress regularly and adjust your plan as needed.
- **Avoid Lifestyle Inflation**: Resist the temptation to increase your spending as your income rises. Focus on saving and investing instead.

Maximizing Savings

- **High-Interest Savings Accounts**: Use high-interest savings accounts to earn more on your extra income.
- **Invest Wisely**: Consider investing extra income to grow your wealth over time.
- **Reduce Unnecessary Expenses**: Review your budget and identify areas where you can cut costs to save more.

By exploring part-time job opportunities, freelancing, and gig economy options, venturing into online money-making activities, turning hobbies into income, and implementing effective saving strategies, you can significantly boost your income and accelerate your journey towards financial goals. These steps will not only provide you with additional financial resources but also enhance your skills, network, and overall financial stability.

Part II: Mastering the Art of Spending

Chapter 05

Smart Shopping and Saving

Spending wisely is just as important as earning and saving money. Mastering the art of spending involves understanding the psychology behind consumer behavior, learning techniques to find the best deals, and adopting habits that minimize unnecessary purchases. This chapter will cover the psychology of consumerism, comparison shopping, avoiding impulse purchases, using coupons and loyalty programs, and building a capsule wardrobe to minimize spending.

The Psychology of Consumerism

Understanding Consumer Behavior

Consumer behavior is influenced by various psychological factors that can drive spending habits. By understanding these factors, you can make more informed and rational purchasing decisions.

Key Psychological Factors

- **Emotional Spending**: Buying items to fulfill emotional needs, such as stress relief or happiness.
- **Social Influence**: Purchasing items to fit in with peers or conform to social norms.
- **Marketing and Advertising**: Persuasive advertising techniques that create a sense of urgency or desire.
- **Scarcity Principle**: The belief that scarce items are more valuable, leading to impulsive buying.
- **Reward Systems**: The brain's reward system triggers pleasure when making purchases, reinforcing the behavior.

Combatting Psychological Triggers

- **Mindful Spending**: Reflect on your motivations before making a purchase. Ask yourself if the item is a want or a need.
- **Delay Gratification**: Wait 24 hours before making a purchase. This helps reduce impulse buying.
- **Set Spending Limits**: Establish a budget for discretionary spending to avoid overspending.
- **Focus on Needs Over Wants**: Prioritize essential purchases and limit spending on non-essential items.

Comparison Shopping and Finding Deals

Benefits of Comparison Shopping

Comparison shopping involves researching different retailers and prices before making a purchase. It helps you find the best deals and avoid overpaying.

Steps for Effective Comparison Shopping

1. **Identify the Product**: Determine the exact product you want to buy.
2. **Research Prices**: Use online tools and websites to compare prices from different retailers.
3. **Check Reviews**: Read customer reviews to ensure the product meets your expectations.
4. **Look for Discounts**: Search for discount codes, sales, and promotions.
5. **Evaluate Total Cost**: Consider additional costs like shipping and taxes.

Tools and Websites for Comparison Shopping

- **Google Shopping**: Aggregates product listings from various retailers.
- **PriceGrabber**: Compares prices from multiple online stores.
- **CamelCamelCamel**: Tracks price history on Amazon to find the best time to buy.
- **RetailMeNot**: Offers coupons and discount codes for numerous retailers.
- **Honey**: A browser extension that automatically applies the best coupon codes at checkout.

Avoiding Impulse Purchases

Understanding Impulse Purchases

Impulse purchases are unplanned buys driven by immediate desires rather than needs. They can quickly derail your budget and savings goals.

Strategies to Avoid Impulse Purchases

1. **Create a Shopping List**: Stick to a list of necessary items when shopping.
2. **Set a Waiting Period**: Implement a 24-hour rule before buying non-essential items.
3. **Limit Exposure**: Avoid browsing stores or websites when you don't need to buy anything.
4. **Use Cash**: Paying with cash can make you more aware of your spending compared to using credit cards.
5. **Unsubscribe from Marketing Emails**: Reduce temptation by unsubscribing from promotional emails.

The Benefits of Avoiding Impulse Purchases

- **Financial Savings**: Save money by only buying what you need.
- **Reduced Clutter**: Minimize unnecessary items in your home.
- **Increased Financial Control**: Stay on track with your budget and financial goals.

Using Coupons and Loyalty Programs

The Advantages of Coupons and Loyalty Programs

Coupons and loyalty programs can provide significant savings on everyday purchases. They reward regular customers and incentivize smart shopping.

Types of Coupons

- **Manufacturer Coupons**: Offered by product manufacturers and can be used at various retailers.
- **Store Coupons**: Issued by specific stores and valid only at those locations.
- **Digital Coupons**: Available online or through retailer apps and can be applied at checkout.

How to Use Coupons Effectively

1. **Collect Coupons**: Gather coupons from newspapers, websites, and store apps.
2. **Organize Coupons**: Keep coupons organized by expiration date and category.

3. **Combine Coupons**: Use manufacturer and store coupons together for maximum savings.
4. **Shop Sales**: Pair coupons with store sales for additional discounts.
5. **Track Expirations**: Use coupons before they expire to avoid missing out on savings.

Benefits of Loyalty Programs

- **Exclusive Discounts**: Access special deals and promotions available only to members.
- **Rewards Points**: Earn points for purchases that can be redeemed for discounts or free items.
- **Personalized Offers**: Receive tailored deals based on your shopping habits.
- **Early Access**: Get early access to sales and new product releases.

Popular Loyalty Programs

- **Grocery Stores**: Programs like Kroger Plus, Safeway Club, and Publix Club.
- **Retail Stores**: Programs like Target Circle, Kohl's Rewards, and Macy's Star Rewards.
- **Online Retailers**: Programs like Amazon Prime, eBay Bucks, and Rakuten.

Building a Capsule Wardrobe and Minimizing Purchases

What is a Capsule Wardrobe?

A capsule wardrobe is a collection of essential clothing items that can be mixed and matched to create a variety of outfits. It focuses on quality over quantity and aims to minimize unnecessary purchases.

Benefits of a Capsule Wardrobe

- **Simplicity**: Reduces decision fatigue by limiting outfit choices.
- **Cost Savings**: Saves money by focusing on versatile, timeless pieces rather than trendy items.
- **Sustainability**: Promotes eco-friendly fashion by reducing consumption.
- **Organization**: Creates a more organized and manageable closet.

How to Build a Capsule Wardrobe

1. **Assess Your Style**: Identify your personal style and the types of clothing you wear most often.
2. **Choose a Color Palette**: Select a cohesive color scheme to ensure all items can be easily mixed and matched.
3. **Select Key Pieces**: Invest in high-quality basics like jeans, t-shirts, blazers, and dresses.
4. **Limit Accessories**: Choose versatile accessories that complement multiple outfits.
5. **Evaluate Seasonally**: Adjust your capsule wardrobe seasonally to accommodate weather changes and trends.

Minimizing Purchases

1. **Focus on Quality**: Invest in high-quality items that last longer rather than cheap, disposable fashion.

2. **Avoid Fast Fashion**: Steer clear of trendy, low-quality items that quickly go out of style.
3. **Mindful Shopping**: Only buy items that complement your existing wardrobe and serve a purpose.
4. **Secondhand Shopping**: Consider thrift stores and online resale platforms for sustainable fashion options.

By understanding the psychology of consumerism, practicing comparison shopping, avoiding impulse purchases, utilizing coupons and loyalty programs, and building a capsule wardrobe, you can master the art of smart shopping and saving. These strategies will help you make informed purchasing decisions, maximize your savings, and achieve greater financial stability while enjoying the things you need and love.

Chapter 06

Dining Out and Entertainment on a Budget

Entertainment and dining out are enjoyable parts of life, but they can quickly add up and strain your budget if not managed carefully. This chapter explores strategies for enjoying dining and entertainment without overspending. We'll cover cooking at home and meal planning, finding free or low-cost entertainment, sharing costs with friends, setting entertainment limits, and avoiding credit card debt from entertainment spending.

Cooking at Home and Meal Planning

Benefits of Cooking at Home

- **Cost Savings**: Preparing meals at home is generally much cheaper than dining out.
- **Healthier Options**: Control over ingredients and portion sizes leads to healthier eating.
- **Skill Development**: Cooking is a valuable life skill that can be enjoyable and rewarding.
- **Family Bonding**: Cooking and dining together can strengthen family relationships.

Tips for Successful Meal Planning

1. **Plan Weekly Meals**: Dedicate time each week to plan meals and create a shopping list.
2. **Use Sales and Coupons**: Base your meal plans on items that are on sale or for which you have coupons.
3. **Cook in Batches**: Prepare large quantities of food and store leftovers for future meals.
4. **Use Versatile Ingredients**: Choose ingredients that can be used in multiple recipes.

5. **Prep in Advance**: Prepare ingredients ahead of time to streamline cooking during the week.

Simple and Budget-Friendly Recipes

- **Pasta Dishes**: Versatile and quick to prepare, pasta can be combined with a variety of sauces and vegetables.
- **Stir-Fries**: Use fresh or frozen vegetables and a protein source like chicken, beef, or tofu.
- **Soups and Stews**: Hearty and filling, soups can be made in large batches and frozen for later use.
- **Salads**: Incorporate greens, proteins, and a variety of toppings for a nutritious and budget-friendly meal.

Finding Free or Low-Cost Entertainment

Enjoying the Outdoors

- **Parks and Trails**: Explore local parks, hiking trails, and nature reserves.
- **Beaches and Lakes**: Spend a day at the beach or by the lake for a relaxing and inexpensive outing.
- **Picnics**: Pack a meal and enjoy a picnic in a scenic location.

Community Events

- **Festivals and Fairs**: Many communities host free or low-cost festivals and fairs with food, music, and activities.
- **Concerts and Performances**: Look for free concerts, theater performances, and art shows in your area.

- **Library Events**: Libraries often offer free events such as book readings, workshops, and movie nights.
- **At-Home Entertainment**
- **Movie Nights**: Stream movies at home instead of going to the theater.
- **Game Nights**: Host a game night with friends or family using board games or video games.
- **DIY Projects**: Engage in do-it-yourself projects or crafts that interest you.

Sharing Costs with Friends

Group Discounts and Deals

- **Group Rates**: Many attractions and events offer discounts for group bookings.
- **Sharing Subscriptions**: Share the cost of streaming services or other subscriptions with friends or family.

Potluck Gatherings

- **Potluck Dinners**: Organize potluck dinners where everyone brings a dish to share, reducing the overall cost.
- **Themed Nights**: Host themed nights, such as taco night or pizza night, where each person contributes ingredients.

Carpooling and Ride Sharing

- **Carpooling**: Share rides to events or outings to save on transportation costs.
- **Ride-Sharing Apps**: Use ride-sharing services and split the fare with friends.

Setting Entertainment Limits

Creating an Entertainment Budget

1. **Assess Your Finances**: Determine how much you can reasonably allocate to entertainment without compromising other financial goals.
2. **Set a Monthly Limit**: Establish a monthly spending limit for entertainment and dining out.
3. **Track Expenses**: Use budgeting apps or spreadsheets to monitor your spending and ensure you stay within your limits.
4. **Prioritize Activities**: Decide which entertainment activities are most important to you and allocate funds accordingly.

Being Mindful of Spending

- **Plan Ahead**: Plan entertainment activities in advance to avoid spontaneous and potentially costly decisions.
- **Look for Deals**: Always search for discounts, coupons, and deals before making entertainment plans.
- **Limit Frequency**: Reduce the frequency of dining out or expensive outings to stay within your budget.

Avoiding Credit Card Debt from Entertainment Spending

The Dangers of Relying on Credit

Using credit cards for entertainment can lead to debt if not managed responsibly. Interest charges can accumulate quickly, making it harder to pay off balances.

Strategies to Avoid Credit Card Debt

1. **Use Cash or Debit**: Pay for entertainment expenses with cash or a debit card to avoid overspending.
2. **Set Spending Alerts**: Use your bank's alert system to notify you when you reach a certain spending limit.
3. **Pay Off Balances Monthly**: If you use a credit card, make sure to pay off the balance in full each month to avoid interest charges.
4. **Avoid Impulse Buys**: Stick to your entertainment budget and avoid impulsive credit card purchases.

Benefits of Responsible Credit Use

- **Builds Credit History**: Responsible credit card use can help build a positive credit history and improve your credit score.
- **Rewards and Benefits**: Some credit cards offer rewards, cashback, or other benefits that can be advantageous if used wisely.
- **Emergency Backup**: A credit card can be useful for emergencies, but it should not be relied upon for regular expenses.

By implementing these strategies, you can enjoy dining out and entertainment without compromising your financial stability.

Cooking at home, finding free or low-cost entertainment, sharing costs with friends, setting entertainment limits, and avoiding credit card debt will help you maintain a balanced and enjoyable lifestyle while staying on track with your financial goals.

Chapter 07

Managing Debt and Building Credit

Managing debt and building good credit are essential components of financial health. In this chapter, we will explore the different types of debt, how to create an effective debt repayment plan, the basics of building good credit, avoiding common credit card pitfalls, and protecting your credit score.

Understanding Different Types of Debt

Types of Debt

1. **Secured Debt**: Loans that are backed by collateral, such as a mortgage or auto loan. If you fail to repay the loan, the lender can seize the collateral.
2. **Unsecured Debt**: Loans that are not backed by collateral, such as credit cards and personal loans. These typically have higher interest rates because they pose a higher risk to lenders.
3. **Revolving Debt**: Credit that is automatically renewed as debts are paid off. The most common example is credit card debt.
4. **Installment Debt**: Loans repaid with fixed payments over a specified period, such as student loans and car loans.

Understanding Interest Rates

Interest rates significantly impact the cost of debt. Here are key concepts to understand:

- **Annual Percentage Rate (APR)**: The annual cost of borrowing expressed as a percentage. It includes interest and fees.

- **Fixed Interest Rate**: An interest rate that remains constant throughout the life of the loan.
- **Variable Interest Rate**: An interest rate that can change based on market conditions.

The Impact of Debt on Financial Health

Carrying debt can affect your financial stability and future borrowing ability. It's crucial to manage debt wisely to avoid financial strain.

Creating a Debt Repayment Plan

Assess Your Debt

1. **List Your Debts**: Write down all your debts, including the creditor, total amount owed, interest rate, and minimum monthly payment.
2. **Calculate Your Debt-to-Income Ratio**: This ratio helps you understand your debt load relative to your income. Calculate it by dividing your total monthly debt payments by your gross monthly income.

Repayment Strategies

1. **Debt Snowball Method**: Focus on paying off the smallest debt first while making minimum payments on other debts. Once the smallest debt is paid, move to the next smallest.
2. **Debt Avalanche Method**: Focus on paying off the debt with the highest interest rate first while making minimum payments on other debts. This method saves money on interest over time.

3. **Debt Consolidation**: Combine multiple debts into a single loan with a lower interest rate. This can simplify payments and reduce interest costs.
4. **Balance Transfer**: Transfer high-interest credit card debt to a card with a lower interest rate. Be mindful of transfer fees and the duration of the lower rate.

Creating a Budget

1. **Track Income and Expenses**: Create a detailed budget to track your income and expenses. Identify areas where you can cut costs to allocate more money toward debt repayment.
2. **Set Goals**: Establish clear, achievable goals for paying off your debts. Having a timeline can keep you motivated and on track.
3. **Automate Payments**: Set up automatic payments to ensure you never miss a due date, which can help you avoid late fees and damage to your credit score.

Building Good Credit: The Basics

Understanding Credit Scores

Your credit score is a numerical representation of your creditworthiness. The most commonly used credit score is the FICO score, which ranges from 300 to 850.

Factors Affecting Your Credit Score

- **Payment History**: Timely payments positively impact your score, while late or missed payments can lower it.
- **Credit Utilization**: The ratio of your current credit card balances to your credit limits. Keeping this ratio below 30% is recommended.
- **Length of Credit History**: Longer credit histories generally improve your score.
- **Credit Mix**: Having a mix of credit types (credit cards, installment loans, etc.) can positively affect your score.
- **New Credit**: Opening several new credit accounts in a short period can lower your score.

Steps to Build Good Credit

1. **Open a Credit Card**: Start with a secured credit card if you have no credit history. Use it responsibly to build a positive credit history.
2. **Pay Bills on Time**: Consistently make on-time payments for all bills, including utilities, rent, and loans.
3. **Keep Balances Low**: Maintain low balances on credit cards and revolving credit accounts.
4. **Monitor Your Credit Report**: Regularly check your credit report for errors and dispute any inaccuracies.

Avoiding Credit Card Pitfalls

Common Credit Card Mistakes

1. **Carrying High Balances**: High balances can lead to high interest charges and negatively impact your credit score.
2. **Making Minimum Payments Only**: Paying only the minimum extends the repayment period and increases the total interest paid.
3. **Ignoring Terms and Conditions**: Failing to understand the terms can lead to unexpected fees and interest rate increases.
4. **Applying for Too Many Cards**: Multiple credit inquiries within a short time can lower your credit score.

Responsible Credit Card Use

1. **Pay in Full Each Month**: Avoid interest charges by paying off your balance in full every month.
2. **Use for Necessary Purchases Only**: Avoid using credit cards for unnecessary or impulsive purchases.
3. **Understand Fees**: Be aware of all fees associated with your credit card, including annual fees, late payment fees, and foreign transaction fees.
4. **Set Spending Limits**: Establish personal spending limits to avoid overextending yourself.

Protecting Your Credit Score

Monitoring Your Credit

1. **Regularly Check Credit Reports**: Obtain free credit reports annually from the three major credit bureaus (Experian, Equifax, and TransUnion) at AnnualCreditReport.com.

2. **Use Credit Monitoring Services**: Consider using credit monitoring services that alert you to changes in your credit report.

Protecting Against Identity Theft

1. **Safeguard Personal Information**: Be cautious with personal information, both online and offline. Shred sensitive documents and use secure passwords.
2. **Monitor Account Activity**: Regularly review bank and credit card statements for unauthorized transactions.
3. **Report Fraud Immediately**: If you suspect fraud, report it to your bank, credit card issuer, and credit bureaus immediately.

Managing Debt Collections

1. **Communicate with Creditors**: If you're struggling to make payments, communicate with your creditors to discuss potential solutions, such as payment plans or hardship programs.
2. **Understand Your Rights**: Familiarize yourself with your rights under the Fair Debt Collection Practices Act (FDCPA), which protects against abusive debt collection practices.

Managing debt and building good credit are foundational elements of financial health. By understanding the different types of debt, creating a strategic debt repayment plan, building and maintaining good credit, avoiding common credit card pitfalls, and protecting your credit score, you can achieve greater financial stability and set yourself up for a prosperous financial future. These practices will not only help you manage your current financial obligations but also pave the way for future financial opportunities and success.

Part III: Investing for Your Future

Chapter 08

Investing Basics: Understanding the Market

Investing is a crucial aspect of building wealth and securing your financial future. This chapter delves into the fundamentals of investing, distinguishing between saving and investing, understanding diversification, the differences between long-term and short-term investing, the relationship between risk and return, and the significant advantage of starting early in investing.

The Difference Between Saving and Investing

Saving

Saving involves setting aside money in safe, accessible accounts such as savings accounts or certificates of deposit (CDs). The goal is to preserve capital and maintain liquidity, often earning modest interest rates.

Investing

Investing, on the other hand, involves putting money into assets with the expectation of generating returns over time. Investments carry varying degrees of risk and potential for higher returns compared to saving.

Diversification: Spreading Your Investments

Importance of Diversification

Diversification involves spreading investments across different asset classes, industries, and geographic regions to reduce risk.

- **Asset Classes**: Allocate investments among stocks, bonds, real estate, and alternative investments.
- **Industry Sectors**: Invest in diverse sectors such as technology, healthcare, and consumer goods.
- **Geographic Regions**: Consider international investments to diversify geopolitical risk.

Long-Term vs. Short-Term Investing

Long-Term Investing

Long-term investing typically spans years to decades, aiming to achieve substantial growth and withstand market fluctuations. Common long-term investments include retirement accounts (e.g., 401(k) or IRA) and equity investments.

Short-Term Investing

Short-term investing focuses on achieving quick profits over a shorter period. Examples include trading stocks, flipping real estate, and investing in short-term bonds or money market funds.

The Role of Risk and Return

Risk

Risk refers to the potential for investment losses due to market volatility, economic downturns, or specific risks associated with individual investments (e.g., company bankruptcy).

- **Types of Risk**: Systematic risk (market-wide), unsystematic risk (specific to individual investments), inflation risk, and interest rate risk.

Return

Return is the gain or loss on an investment over a specified period. Higher risk investments typically offer higher potential returns, while lower risk investments offer lower returns.

- **Types of Returns**: Capital gains (profits from selling investments), dividends (income from stocks), interest (income from bonds or savings accounts).

Starting Early: The Power of Time

Importance of Early Investing

Starting to invest early provides significant advantages due to the power of compounding and long-term growth potential.

- **Compounding**: Earning returns on both the initial investment and accumulated earnings over time.
- **Time Horizon**: Longer investment periods allow for greater resilience against market fluctuations and potential to recover from losses.

Strategies for Effective Investing

Determine Investment Goals

1. **Short-Term Goals**: Allocate funds for immediate needs or anticipated expenses within the next 1-5 years.
2. **Long-Term Goals**: Plan for major life events such as retirement, education funding, or wealth accumulation over decades.

Asset Allocation

1. **Risk Tolerance**: Assess your risk tolerance based on financial goals, time horizon, and comfort level with market fluctuations.
2. **Diversification**: Spread investments across different asset classes to mitigate risk and optimize returns.

Investment Vehicles

1. **Stocks**: Ownership shares in companies, offering potential for capital appreciation and dividends.
2. **Bonds**: Debt securities issued by governments or corporations, providing regular interest payments and return of principal at maturity.
3. **Mutual Funds and ETFs**: Pooled investments that offer diversification across multiple securities or asset classes.
4. **Real Estate**: Direct ownership or through Real Estate Investment Trusts (REITs), offering rental income and potential property appreciation.
5. **Retirement Accounts**: Tax-advantaged accounts like 401(k)s or IRAs designed for long-term savings and investment growth.

Tools and Resources for Investors

Research and Analysis

1. **Financial Websites**: Access financial news, market analysis, and investment research on platforms like Bloomberg, CNBC, and Yahoo Finance.
2. **Brokerage Accounts**: Use online brokerage platforms to buy and sell investments, with access to research tools and educational resources.

Financial Advisors

1. **Certified Financial Planners (CFPs)**: Seek advice from professionals who can provide personalized investment strategies aligned with your goals and risk tolerance.
2. **Robo-Advisors**: Automated investment platforms that create and manage diversified portfolios based on your financial goals and risk profile.

Understanding the basics of investing is essential for achieving financial goals and building long-term wealth. By distinguishing between saving and investing, practicing diversification, understanding risk and return dynamics, and leveraging the power of compounding through early investments, individuals can make informed decisions to secure their financial futures. Start early, diversify wisely, and stay informed to maximize the potential benefits of investing while managing risks effectively.

Chapter 09

Stocks, Bonds, and Mutual Funds: A Beginner's Guide

Investing in stocks, bonds, and mutual funds offers a variety of options for building wealth and achieving financial goals. This chapter serves as a beginner's guide to understanding stocks and the stock market, investing in bonds as a low-risk option, utilizing mutual funds for diversification, exploring index funds for a straightforward investment approach, and conducting research and due diligence before making investment decisions.

Understanding Stocks and the Stock Market

What are Stocks?

Stocks represent ownership in a company and are traded on stock exchanges such as the New York Stock Exchange (NYSE) or NASDAQ. Investors purchase stocks to participate in a company's growth and profitability.

Types of Stocks

- **Common Stocks**: Offer voting rights and potential for dividends and capital appreciation.
- **Preferred Stocks**: Prioritize dividend payments over common stocks but may not offer voting rights.

Investing in Stocks

Benefits of Investing in Stocks

- **Potential for Growth**: Stocks historically offer higher returns compared to other asset classes over the long term.

- **Dividend Income**: Some stocks pay regular dividends to shareholders.
- **Portfolio Diversification**: Stocks provide diversification when combined with bonds and other investments.

Risks of Investing in Stocks

- **Volatility**: Stock prices can fluctuate widely due to market conditions, economic factors, or company-specific events.
- **Market Risk**: The overall market performance affects stock prices.
- **Individual Company Risk**: Company-specific issues can impact stock value.

The Stock Market

How the Stock Market Works

- **Stock Exchanges**: Platforms where stocks are bought and sold, facilitating liquidity and price discovery.
- **Stock Indices**: Measure the performance of a group of stocks, such as the S&P 500 or Dow Jones Industrial Average (DJIA).

Strategies for Investing in Stocks

- **Long-Term Investing**: Hold stocks for years to benefit from compounding and potential growth.
- **Value Investing**: Seek undervalued stocks with strong fundamentals for potential capital appreciation.

- **Dividend Investing**: Focus on stocks that pay regular dividends as a source of income.

Investing in Bonds: A Low-Risk Option

What are Bonds?

Bonds are debt securities issued by governments, municipalities, or corporations to raise capital. Investors lend money to the issuer in exchange for regular interest payments (coupon) and repayment of the principal at maturity.

Types of Bonds

- **Government Bonds**: Issued by national governments, considered low-risk due to sovereign backing.
- **Corporate Bonds**: Issued by corporations to raise capital, offering higher yields but with varying degrees of risk.
- **Municipal Bonds**: Issued by state or local governments, often providing tax-exempt income for investors.

Benefits of Investing in Bonds

- **Income Generation**: Bonds provide predictable interest income through regular coupon payments.
- **Capital Preservation**: Generally considered less volatile than stocks, offering stability to investment portfolios.
- **Diversification**: Bonds complement stocks by reducing overall portfolio risk.

Risks of Investing in Bonds

- **Interest Rate Risk**: Bond prices and yields move inversely with interest rate changes.
- **Credit Risk**: Risk of issuer defaulting on payments, particularly with lower-rated bonds (high-yield or junk bonds).
- **Inflation Risk**: Inflation erodes the purchasing power of bond income over time.

Strategies for Investing in Bonds

- **Determine Investment Goals**: Choose bonds that align with your financial objectives, such as income generation or capital preservation.
- **Evaluate Credit Quality**: Assess issuer credit ratings and financial health to gauge bond repayment ability.
- **Consider Duration**: Longer-term bonds may offer higher yields but are more sensitive to interest rate changes.

Mutual Funds: Diversification Made Easy

What are Mutual Funds?

Mutual funds pool money from multiple investors to invest in a diversified portfolio of stocks, bonds, or other securities managed by professional fund managers.

Types of Mutual Funds

- **Equity Funds**: Invest primarily in stocks, aiming for capital appreciation.

- **Bond Funds**: Focus on bonds to provide income and capital preservation.
- **Balanced Funds**: Allocate investments across stocks and bonds for balanced risk and return.

Benefits of Mutual Funds

- **Diversification**: Spread investment risk across multiple securities within a single fund.
- **Professional Management**: Experienced fund managers make investment decisions based on research and market analysis.
- **Accessibility**: Investors can start with relatively small amounts and benefit from diversified portfolios.

Risks of Mutual Funds

- **Market Risk**: Mutual fund performance is influenced by overall market conditions.
- **Management Risk**: Poor investment decisions by fund managers can impact fund performance.
- **Fees and Expenses**: Management fees and operating expenses reduce investor returns.

Index Funds: A Simple Investment Approach

What are Index Funds?

Index funds replicate the performance of a specific market index, such as the S&P 500 or NASDAQ-100, by investing in all or a representative sample of the index's constituent stocks.

Benefits of Index Funds

- **Low Costs**: Index funds typically have lower expense ratios compared to actively managed funds.
- **Diversification**: Mirror the performance of broad market indices, providing exposure to various sectors and companies.
- **Passive Management**: Require minimal trading and oversight, reducing management fees and expenses.

Considerations for Index Funds

- **Tracking Error**: Variations in performance compared to the index due to fund expenses or imperfect replication.
- **Market Volatility**: Index funds are subject to market fluctuations and economic conditions affecting index performance.

Research and Due Diligence

Conducting Research

Fundamental Analysis

- **Financial Statements**: Analyze company financials, including income statements, balance sheets, and cash flow statements.
- **Management Team**: Assess the competence and track record of company executives.
- **Industry Trends**: Understand market dynamics and competitive landscape affecting company performance.

Technical Analysis

- **Price Trends**: Analyze historical price movements and trading volumes using charts and technical indicators.
- **Market Sentiment**: Evaluate investor sentiment and market psychology influencing stock prices.

Due Diligence

Evaluate Investment Risks

- **Risk Assessment**: Consider factors like economic conditions, regulatory changes, and geopolitical events impacting investments.
- **Risk Tolerance**: Align investment choices with your risk tolerance and financial goals.

Review Investment Objectives

- **Long-Term vs. Short-Term Goals**: Choose investments that match your investment horizon and financial objectives.
- **Asset Allocation**: Diversify investments across asset classes to optimize risk-adjusted returns.

Understanding stocks, bonds, mutual funds, and index funds provides a solid foundation for beginner investors seeking to build wealth and achieve financial goals. By grasping the principles of each investment type, conducting thorough research and due diligence, and aligning investments with personal financial objectives and risk tolerance, investors can make informed decisions to navigate the complexities of the financial markets effectively. Start with a clear understanding, proceed with thoughtful analysis, and strive for diversified, well-informed investment strategies to pave the way for long-term financial success.

Chapter 10

Retirement Planning: Starting Early Pays Off

Planning for retirement is crucial for achieving financial independence and security in later years. This chapter explores the essentials of retirement planning, including understanding retirement savings accounts such as 401(k) and IRA, maximizing employer match programs, calculating your retirement needs, investing for retirement based on your age, and maintaining consistency with your retirement plan.

Understanding Retirement Savings Accounts (401(k), IRA)

401(k) Plans

What is a 401(k)?

A 401(k) is an employer-sponsored retirement savings plan that allows employees to contribute a portion of their pre-tax salary to investments such as stocks, bonds, and mutual funds. Contributions grow tax-deferred until withdrawn in retirement.

Benefits of 401(k) Plans

- **Tax Advantages**: Contributions are tax-deferred, reducing taxable income in the current year.
- **Employer Match**: Some employers offer matching contributions, effectively providing free money toward retirement savings.
- **Investment Options**: Choose from a range of investment options based on risk tolerance and retirement goals.

Individual Retirement Accounts (IRA)

Types of IRAs

- **Traditional IRA**: Contributions may be tax-deductible, and earnings grow tax-deferred until withdrawal in retirement.
- **Roth IRA**: Contributions are made with after-tax dollars, and withdrawals in retirement are tax-free if certain conditions are met.

Benefits of IRAs

- **Tax Advantages**: Traditional IRAs offer tax-deferred growth, while Roth IRAs provide tax-free withdrawals in retirement.
- **Flexibility**: IRAs allow individuals to choose from various investment options, similar to 401(k) plans.

Employer Match Programs: Free Money!

Understanding Employer Matches

How Employer Matches Work

- **Matching Contributions**: Employers may match a percentage of employee contributions up to a certain limit, effectively increasing retirement savings without additional cost.
- **Vesting**: Understand vesting schedules to ensure you qualify for employer contributions over time.

Maximizing Employer Matches

- **Contribute Enough to Maximize Match**: Contribute at least enough to qualify for the maximum employer match offered to maximize retirement savings.
- **Take Advantage of Catch-Up Contributions**: Individuals aged 50 and older may make additional catch-up contributions to boost retirement savings.

Calculating Your Retirement Needs

Steps to Calculate Retirement Needs

Estimate Retirement Expenses

- **Basic Living Expenses**: Consider housing, utilities, food, and healthcare costs in retirement.
- **Discretionary Expenses**: Plan for travel, hobbies, and other discretionary spending.
- **Inflation Adjustments**: Factor in inflation to estimate future expenses.

Determine Retirement Income Sources

- **Social Security Benefits**: Estimate Social Security income based on earnings history and retirement age.
- **Pension Income**: If applicable, include pension payments as a source of retirement income.
- **Investment Income**: Calculate income from retirement accounts, including 401(k), IRAs, and other investments.

Retirement Savings Gap Analysis

- **Compare Expenses to Income**: Identify any shortfall between estimated expenses and projected income to determine additional savings needed.
- **Adjust Retirement Plan**: Modify contributions and investment strategies to bridge the savings gap and achieve retirement goals.

Investing for Retirement Based on Your Age

Investment Strategies by Age Group

Younger Investors (20s-30s)

- **Higher Risk Tolerance**: Allocate more investments to stocks for long-term growth potential.
- **Long-Term Horizon**: Benefit from compounding and ride out market fluctuations.

Middle-Aged Investors (40s-50s)

- **Balanced Approach**: Shift towards a balanced portfolio with a mix of stocks and bonds to preserve capital and manage risk.
- **Catch-Up Contributions**: Take advantage of catch-up contributions in retirement accounts to accelerate savings.

Pre-Retirees (Late 50s-60s)

- **Conservative Allocation**: Gradually transition investments to more conservative options to protect savings from market volatility.

- **Focus on Income**: Shift focus to generating retirement income through dividends, interest, and stable investments.
- **Staying Consistent with Your Retirement Plan**
- **Strategies for Consistent Retirement Planning**
- **Establish Clear Goals**
- **Set Retirement Age**: Determine when you plan to retire and adjust savings and investments accordingly.
- **Review and Adjust**: Regularly review your retirement plan and make adjustments based on changing financial circumstances or goals.

Automate Contributions

- **Automatic Deductions**: Set up automatic contributions to retirement accounts to ensure consistent savings.
- **Increase Contributions**: Gradually increase contributions over time or with salary increases to accelerate retirement savings.

Monitor and Rebalance Investments

- **Review Portfolio**: Periodically review investment allocations and rebalance to maintain desired asset allocation and risk level.
- **Adjust for Market Changes**: Make strategic adjustments based on market conditions or changes in personal financial goals.

Retirement planning requires careful consideration of retirement savings accounts like 401(k) and IRA, maximizing employer matches, calculating retirement needs, investing based on age-appropriate strategies, and maintaining consistency with your retirement plan. By starting early, taking advantage of employer benefits, estimating retirement expenses, aligning investments with age-based risk tolerance, and staying committed to a long-term plan, individuals can build a secure financial future and enjoy retirement with peace of mind. Begin planning today to reap the benefits of early and strategic retirement preparation.

Part IV: Financial Wellness and Beyond

Chapter 11

Financial Literacy and Beyond: Building a Strong Future

Financial literacy is a cornerstone of financial wellness, empowering individuals to make informed decisions and secure their financial futures. This chapter explores the importance of financial education, setting long-term financial goals, creating an emergency fund, protecting yourself with insurance, and giving back to your community for overall financial well-being.

The Importance of Financial Education

Understanding Financial Literacy

Financial literacy encompasses the knowledge and skills needed to manage personal finances effectively. It includes budgeting, saving, investing, managing debt, and understanding financial products and services.

Benefits of Financial Education

- **Empowerment**: Enables individuals to make informed financial decisions and avoid common pitfalls.
- **Improved Financial Well-Being**: Leads to better financial outcomes, including increased savings, reduced debt, and improved credit scores.
- **Long-Term Security**: Builds a foundation for long-term financial stability and retirement readiness.

Setting Long-Term Financial Goals

Benefits of Goal Setting

- **Clarity and Focus**: Establishing clear financial goals provides direction and motivation for financial planning.
- **Prioritization**: Helps prioritize spending and savings decisions based on long-term objectives.
- **Measurement of Progress**: Allows tracking progress towards goals and making necessary adjustments.

Types of Financial Goals

1. **Short-Term Goals**: Achievable within 1-3 years, such as building an emergency fund or paying off credit card debt.
2. **Medium-Term Goals**: Attainable within 3-5 years, such as saving for a down payment on a home or funding higher education.
3. **Long-Term Goals**: Targets set for 5 years or more, such as retirement savings, investment portfolios, or estate planning.

Creating an Emergency Fund

Importance of an Emergency Fund

An emergency fund serves as a financial safety net, providing funds to cover unexpected expenses or income disruptions without resorting to debt.

How Much to Save

- **Guidelines**: Aim to save 3-6 months' worth of living expenses in your emergency fund.
- **Factors to Consider**: Consider personal circumstances, such as job stability, family size, and

health expenses, when determining the appropriate fund size.

Building an Emergency Fund

1. **Automate Savings**: Set up automatic transfers from your paycheck or checking account to a separate savings account dedicated to emergencies.
2. **Prioritize Savings**: Allocate a portion of your monthly budget specifically towards building and replenishing your emergency fund.
3. **Use Windfalls Wisely**: Direct unexpected windfalls, such as tax refunds or bonuses, towards your emergency fund to accelerate savings.

Protecting Yourself with Insurance

Importance of Insurance

Insurance provides financial protection against unforeseen events that could lead to significant financial loss, such as illness, accidents, or property damage.

Types of Insurance Coverage

1. **Health Insurance**: Covers medical expenses and healthcare costs, reducing out-of-pocket expenses for illness or injury.
2. **Auto Insurance**: Protects against financial losses due to vehicle accidents, theft, or damage.
3. **Homeowners or Renters Insurance**: Covers property damage, theft, and liability in rental or owned homes.

4. **Life Insurance**: Provides financial support to beneficiaries in the event of the policyholder's death, ensuring financial security for dependents.
5. **Disability Insurance**: Replaces a portion of lost income if you become unable to work due to injury or illness.

Giving Back to Your Community

Importance of Giving Back

Contributing to your community through volunteer work or charitable donations not only benefits others but also enhances personal fulfillment and social responsibility.

Ways to Give Back

1. **Volunteerism**: Donate time and skills to local charities, schools, or community organizations addressing social needs.
2. **Financial Contributions**: Support causes and nonprofits financially through donations or fundraising efforts.
3. **Corporate Giving Programs**: Participate in employer-sponsored volunteer days or donation matching programs to amplify impact.

Personal Benefits

- **Sense of Purpose**: Contributing to community well-being fosters a sense of purpose and fulfillment.

- **Building Relationships**: Connect with like-minded individuals and build social networks through community involvement.
- **Positive Impact**: Make a meaningful difference in addressing societal challenges and promoting positive change.

Financial literacy and wellness extend beyond personal finances to encompass broader aspects of well-being, including goal setting, emergency preparedness, insurance protection, and community engagement. By prioritizing financial education, setting clear goals, building emergency savings, securing adequate insurance coverage, and giving back to your community, individuals can achieve holistic financial wellness and contribute positively to society. Start today to build a strong foundation for a secure and fulfilling future, guided by principles of financial literacy and responsible citizenship.

Chapter 12

Navigating Financial Challenges and Building Resilience

Financial challenges are inevitable, but with resilience and proactive strategies, individuals can navigate setbacks effectively. This chapter explores methods for dealing with financial setbacks, the significance of financial support systems, avoiding scams, cultivating a healthy relationship with money, and building lasting financial confidence.

Dealing with Financial Setbacks

Understanding Financial Setbacks

Financial setbacks can arise from unexpected events such as job loss, medical emergencies, or economic downturns, impacting income and financial stability.

Strategies for Managing Setbacks

- **Assess the Situation**: Evaluate the extent of the setback and its immediate financial implications.
- **Create a Contingency Plan**: Develop a plan to address immediate financial needs and mitigate long-term impact.
- **Seek Professional Advice**: Consult financial advisors or counselors for guidance on managing financial challenges.

The Importance of Financial Support Systems

Building a Support Network

Types of Financial Support Systems

- **Family and Friends**: Seek emotional and financial support from trusted individuals during times of need.
- **Professional Networks**: Engage with financial advisors, mentors, or support groups for guidance and advice.
- **Community Resources**: Access local organizations or government programs offering financial assistance or counseling services.

Benefits of Support Systems

- **Emotional Resilience**: Receive encouragement and practical assistance to cope with financial stress.
- **Financial Guidance**: Access expertise and resources to make informed decisions and navigate challenges effectively.

Avoiding Financial Scams

Recognizing Common Scams

Types of Financial Scams

- **Phishing and Identity Theft**: Fraudulent attempts to obtain personal or financial information through deceptive means.
- **Investment Scams**: Promises of high returns with little risk, often targeting unsuspecting investors.
- **Charity Scams**: False solicitations for donations to fake charities or causes.

Strategies to Avoid Scams

- **Verify Sources**: Verify the legitimacy of individuals or organizations before sharing personal or financial information.
- **Exercise Caution Online**: Avoid clicking on suspicious links or responding to unsolicited requests for money or personal details.
- **Educate Yourself**: Stay informed about common scams and warning signs to protect against financial fraud.

Cultivating a Healthy Relationship with Money

Developing Financial Mindfulness

Understanding Money Attitudes

- **Money as a Tool**: View money as a means to achieve financial goals and enhance quality of life.
- **Emotional Impact**: Recognize emotional triggers related to spending, saving, or investing decisions.

Strategies for Healthy Money Management

- **Budgeting**: Track income and expenses to maintain financial balance and prioritize spending.
- **Saving Habits**: Establish regular savings goals and automate contributions to build financial security.
- **Long-Term Planning**: Set clear financial goals aligned with personal values and future aspirations.

Building Financial Confidence for Life

Enhancing Financial Literacy

Continuous Learning and Growth

- **Educational Resources**: Access workshops, courses, or online resources to improve financial knowledge and skills.
- **Personal Finance Tools**: Utilize budgeting apps, investment calculators, or retirement planning tools for informed decision-making.

Overcoming Financial Challenges

- **Resilience**: Develop resilience to bounce back from setbacks and adapt to changing financial circumstances.
- **Goal Achievement**: Celebrate milestones and achievements along the journey to financial independence and stability.

Navigating financial challenges requires resilience, proactive planning, and leveraging support systems to overcome setbacks effectively. By understanding strategies for managing financial setbacks, building strong support networks, avoiding scams, cultivating a healthy relationship with money, and continuously enhancing financial literacy, individuals can build lasting financial confidence and security. Start today by implementing practical steps and seeking assistance when needed to strengthen financial resilience and achieve long-term financial well-being.

CONCLUSION

In conclusion, mastering personal finance is a journey that empowers individuals to achieve financial independence and build a secure future. Throughout this guidebook, we've explored key financial principles, strategies for creating a personalized financial roadmap, the path to financial independence, the importance of continuous learning and adaptation, and the steps to building a bright financial future. Let's recap the essential elements that pave the way to financial success:

Recap of Key Financial Principles

Financial Literacy

Understanding the fundamentals of money management, including budgeting, saving, investing, and debt management, forms the foundation of financial literacy.

Goal Setting

Setting clear and achievable financial goals provides direction and motivation, whether it's saving for emergencies, purchasing a home, or planning for retirement.

Budgeting and Saving

Creating a budget and tracking expenses helps manage cash flow effectively, while saving consistently builds financial reserves for short-term needs and long-term goals.

Investing Wisely

Learning about investment options, including stocks, bonds, mutual funds, and retirement accounts, allows individuals to grow wealth over time through informed decisions and strategic planning.

Managing Debt

Developing strategies to manage and reduce debt, such as prioritizing high-interest loans and consolidating debt when beneficial, improves financial stability and creditworthiness.

Protecting Assets

Securing adequate insurance coverage, including health, auto, home, and life insurance, safeguards against unexpected expenses and risks, ensuring financial security for individuals and their families.

Creating a Personalized Financial Roadmap

Assessing Financial Situation

Evaluating current financial standing, including income, expenses, assets, and liabilities, provides a clear starting point for developing a personalized financial plan.

Setting Priorities

Identifying short-term, medium-term, and long-term financial goals based on personal values and aspirations helps prioritize financial decisions and allocate resources effectively.

Developing Strategies

Implementing strategies such as budgeting, saving, investing, and debt repayment tailored to individual circumstances and goals ensures progress towards financial objectives.

Monitoring Progress

Regularly reviewing and adjusting the financial plan in response to changing circumstances, economic conditions, or life events supports ongoing financial stability and goal achievement.

The Journey to Financial Independence

Building Wealth

Accumulating wealth through disciplined saving, smart investing, and strategic financial decisions accelerates progress towards financial independence and long-term prosperity.

Achieving Freedom

Attaining financial independence provides the freedom to pursue personal passions, retire comfortably, and navigate life's transitions with confidence and security.

Continuous Learning and Adaptation

Lifelong Learning

Engaging in continuous learning about personal finance, economic trends, and investment strategies enhances financial knowledge and decision-making skills over time.

Adaptability

Remaining flexible and adaptable to evolving financial goals, market conditions, and personal circumstances ensures resilience and long-term financial success.

Building a Bright Financial Future

Long-Term Vision

Maintaining a long-term perspective and staying committed to financial goals fosters perseverance and resilience in achieving financial milestones.

Empowerment and Confidence

Gaining financial knowledge, making informed decisions, and taking proactive steps towards financial security empower individuals to control their financial future confidently.

In conclusion, mastering personal finance requires dedication, education, and a proactive approach to building financial wellness and achieving goals. By embracing key financial principles, creating a personalized financial roadmap, embarking on the journey to financial independence, continuously learning and adapting, and striving to build a bright financial future, individuals can navigate challenges, seize opportunities, and create a life of financial freedom and stability. Start your journey today and pave the way for a prosperous tomorrow.

www.ingramcontent.com/pod-product-compliance
Lightning Source LLC
Chambersburg PA
CBHW071101240526
45471CB00016B/2287